Magnificent Tea Cookbook That You Will Love

The Easiest Iced Tea Recipes That Will Freshen You Up

BY: Valeria Ray

License Notes

Copyright © 2019 Valeria Ray All Rights Reserved

All rights to the content of this book are reserved by the Author without exception unless permission is given stating otherwise.

The Author have no claims as to the authenticity of the content and the Reader bears all responsibility and risk when following the content. The Author is not liable for any reparations, damages, accidents, injuries or other incidents occurring from the Reader following all or part of this publication.

A Special Reward for Purchasing My Book!

Thank you, cherished reader, for purchasing my book and taking the time to read it. As a special reward for your decision, I would like to offer a gift of free and discounted books directly to your inbox. All you need to do is fill in the box below with your email address and name to start getting amazing offers in the comfort of your own home. You will never miss an offer because a reminder will be sent to you. Never miss a deal and get great deals without having to leave the house! Subscribe now and start saving!

https://valeria-ray.gr8.com

Contents

Tasty Iced Tea Recipes 7

(1) Iced Green Tea with Lime 8

(2) Orange Honey Sweet Iced Tea 10

(3) Cold Brew Iced Tea 12

(4) Almond Iced Tea 14

(5) Sweet Lime Iced Tea 16

(6) Apple Spice Iced Tea 18

(7) Russian Iced Tea 20

(8) Arnold Palmer Iced Tea 22

(9) Plum Thyme Iced Tea 24

(10) Basil Nectarine Iced Tea 26

(11) Pineapple Iced Tea 28

(12) Blackberry Minty Sweet Iced Tea 30

(13) Peaches and Cream Iced Tea 33

(14) Blueberry Lemon Iced Tea 35

(15) Minty Tea Punch 38

(16) Cherry Vanilla Iced Tea 40

(17) Minty Peach Iced Tea.. 42

(18) Citrus Iced Tea 44

(19) Minty Iced Green Tea 46

(20) Cranberry Mint Tea Lemonade 48

(21) Mango Iced Tea... 50

(22) Cranberry-Raspberry Tea 53

(23) Lavender Lemon Iced Tea 55

(24) Creamy Chai Iced Tea.. 57

(25) Iced Tea Smoothie 59

(26) Ginger Honey Iced Tea 61

(27) Iced Tea Shake 63

(28) Green Tea Soda 65

(29) Honeydew Mint Iced Tea 67

(30) Herbal Sun Tea... 70

About the Author.. 72

Author's Afterthoughts... 74

Tasty Iced Tea Recipes

MMMMMMMMMMMMMMMMMMMMMMMMMMMMM

(1) Iced Green Tea with Lime

Cooling and satisfying, lime gives this iced green tea the perfect amount of zest and increases healthy antioxidants.

Yield: 2 Quarts

Preparation Time: 15 mins.

List of Ingredients:

- One Quart Hot Water
- 8 teaspoons Green Tea OR
- Green Jasmine Pearls Tea
- Juice from 4 Limes
- Lime Slices for garnish (optional)
- Honey to Taste (optional)
- One Quart Cold Water

MMMMMMMMMMMMMMMMMMMMMMMMMMMMMMMM

Methods:

1. Bring one quart of water to boil. Add loose tea to a tea filter bag and infuse in hot water.
2. Steep tea four minutes. Remove tea in the infuser or bag of tea and discard.
3. Add honey if desired and stir well. Add lime juice and remaining quart of cold water and chill.
4. Serve over ice and garnish with lime slices.

(2) Orange Honey Sweet Iced Tea

A delectable way to serve sweet tea with a burst of fresh orange.

Yield: 2 Quarts

Preparation Time: 15 mins.

List of Ingredients:

- One Quart Hot Water
- 8 teaspoons Black Tea
- 1 Cup Sugar
- 2 Tablespoons Honey
- 1 Orange, Sliced Very Thinly, Seeds Removed
- Mint Leaves for Garnish (optional)
- Cold Water

MMMMMMMMMMMMMMMMMMMMMMMMMMMMMM

Methods:

1. Bring one quart of water to boil. Add loose tea to a tea filter bag and infuse in hot water. Steep tea four minutes.
2. Remove tea leaves in the infuser or bag of tea and discard. Add sugar and honey and stir until dissolved.
3. Add orange slices and enough cold water to make 2 quarts. Stir well. Chill.
4. Serve over ice.

(3) Cold Brew Iced Tea

Cold Brew Iced Tea has a smoother taste than tea made the traditional way and is very easy to do.

Yield: 2 Quarts

Preparation Time: 15 mins.

List of Ingredients:

- 1 Quart Hot Water
- 8 teaspoons Black Tea
- 8 Tablespoons sugar
- 1 Cinnamon Stick
- Freshly separated mint leaves
- ¾ quart Cold Water

MMMMMMMMMMMMMMMMMMMMMMMMMMMMMMMM

Methods:

1. Use your favorite iced tea recipe but do not heat the water.
2. Simply fill infuser or a tea filter bag with desired amount of tea and any other ingredients (i.e., mint leaves, cinnamon stick, etc.) and place in a two-quart mason jar or pitcher filled with water.
3. Refrigerate overnight and then remove tea and discard.
4. Super simple!

(4) Almond Iced Tea

Try Almond Iced Tea for a tasty twist on iced tea!

Yield: 2 Quarts

Preparation Time: 15 mins.

List of Ingredients:

- One Quart Hot Water
- 8 teaspoons Black Tea OR
- English Breakfast Tea
- ½ teaspoons Almond Extract
- Sugar or Simple Syrup, to Taste (optional)
- One Quart Cold Water
- Ice

MMMMMMMMMMMMMMMMMMMMMMMMMMMMMMM

Methods:

1. Bring one quart of water to boil. Add loose tea to a tea filter bag and infuse in hot water.
2. Steep tea four minutes. Remove tea in the infuser or bag of tea and discard.
3. Add sugar if desired (approx. ½ to 1 cup sugar) and stir to dissolve. Add Almond Extract and stir.
4. Chill. Serve in glasses over ice.

(5) Sweet Lime Iced Tea

Invigorating Sweet Lime Iced Tea gives lemonade a run for its money.

Yield: 2 Quarts

Preparation Time: 15 mins.

List of Ingredients:

- One Quart Hot Water
- 8 teaspoons Black Tea
- ¾ Cup White Sugar
- 4 Limes, Juiced
- One Quart Cold Water

MMMMMMMMMMMMMMMMMMMMMMMMMMMMMMM

Methods:

1. Bring one quart of water to boil. Add loose tea to a tea filter bag and infuse in hot water.
2. Steep tea four minutes. Remove tea in the infuser or bag of tea and discard.
3. Stir in sugar and lime juice until sugar is dissolved.
4. Add one quart cold water and stir.
5. Chill and serve over ice.

(6) Apple Spice Iced Tea

Luscious apple cider blends well with lively cinnamon and clove spices.

Yield: 2 Quarts

Preparation Time: 15 mins.

List of Ingredients:

- One Quart Hot Water
- 8 teaspoons Black Tea
- 2 Cups Apple Cider
- 2 Cinnamon Sticks
- 2 teaspoons Whole Cloves
- Cold Water
- Ice

MMMMMMMMMMMMMMMMMMMMMMMMMMMMMM

Methods:

1. Bring one quart of water to boil.
2. Add loose tea, 2 teaspoons whole cloves, and 2 cinnamon sticks to a tea filter bag and infuse in hot water.
3. Steep tea four minutes. Remove tea and spices in the infuser or bag of tea and discard. Add apple cider.
4. Add cold water to make 2 quarts and stir well. Chill.
5. Serve in glasses over ice.

(7) Russian Iced Tea

This tea will give you a shot of Russia.

Yield: 2 Quarts

Preparation Time: 15 mins.

List of Ingredients:

- One Quart Hot Water
- 8 teaspoons Black Tea
- 2 Tablespoons Whole Cloves
- 3 Tablespoons Fresh Orange Zest
- 4 Whole Cinnamon Sticks
- ½ Cup Honey
- ¼ Cup Freshly Squeezed Lemon Juice
- Cold Water

MMMMMMMMMMMMMMMMMMMMMMMMMMMMMMMMM

Methods:

1. Bring one quart of water to boil.
2. Add loose tea, cloves, and cinnamon sticks (may need to break), and orange zest to a tea filter bag and infuse in hot water.
3. Steep tea four minutes. Remove tea in the infuser or bag of tea and discard.
4. Add honey and stir until honey is dissolved. Add lemon juice and cold water to make 2 quarts and stir. Chill.
5. Serve over ice.

(8) Arnold Palmer Iced Tea

This delicious tea is named after a historic iced tea lover who often drank tea after the U.S. Open in 1960.

Yield: 2 Quarts

Preparation Time: 15 mins

List of Ingredients:

- One Quart Hot Water
- 4 teaspoons English Breakfast Tea OR
- Black Tea
- One Quart Lemonade, Chilled

MMMMMMMMMMMMMMMMMMMMMMMMMMMMMMM

Methods:

1. Bring one quart of water to boil. Add loose tea to a tea filter bag and infuse in hot water.
2. Steep tea four minutes. Remove tea in the infuser or bag of tea and discard.
3. Add the quart of chilled lemonade and stir. Chill.
4. Serve in glasses over ice. Garnish with lemon slice if desired.

(9) Plum Thyme Iced Tea

This tea is a soothing blend of plums, tea, and thyme that has a sweet aroma and a delectable taste.

Yield: 2 Quarts

Preparation Time: 15 mins.

List of Ingredients:

- One Quart Hot Water
- 8 teaspoons Black Tea
- 8 Tablespoons Honey
- 2 Plums, Sliced
- 16 Sprigs Fresh Thyme
- One Quart Cold Water

MMMMMMMMMMMMMMMMMMMMMMMMMMMMMMMM

Methods:

1. Bring one quart of water to boil. Add loose tea to a tea filter bag and infuse in hot water.
2. Steep tea four minutes. Remove tea in the infuser or bag of tea and discard.
3. Add honey, plum slices, and sprigs of thyme and stir until honey is dissolved.
4. Add cold water to make 2 quarts and stir. Chill.
5. Serve over ice.

(10) Basil Nectarine Iced Tea

For a unique and refreshing tea, nectarines and basil blend together for a tasty alternative to classic iced tea.

Yield: 2 Quarts

Preparation Time: 15 mins.

List of Ingredients:

- One Quart Hot Water
- 8 teaspoons Black Tea
- 4 Nectarines, Sliced
- 5 – 10 Basil Leaves
- 1/3 Cup Sugar
- Cold Water

MMMMMMMMMMMMMMMMMMMMMMMMMMMMMMMM

Methods:

1. Bring one quart of water to boil. Add loose tea to a tea filter bag and infuse in hot water.
2. Steep tea four minutes. Remove tea in infuser or bag of tea and discard.
3. While tea is steeping, boil one cup of water, 3/4 of the nectarine slices, and sugar.
4. Simmer for 10 minutes, stirring occasionally. Remove from heat and add basil leaves and let sit for 5 minutes, then discard basil leaves.
5. Stir nectarine mixture into tea. Add water to make 2 quarts and chill.
6. Serve in glasses over ice and garnish with remaining ¼ nectarine slices.

(11) Pineapple Iced Tea

Pineapple Iced Tea is a tropical treat!

Yield: 2 Quarts

Preparation Time: 15 mins.

List of Ingredients:

- One Quart Hot Water
- 8 teaspoons Black Tea
- 2 Cups Pineapple Juice
- 1/3 to ½ Cup Sugar, or Simple Syrup to Taste (optional)
- 1 Can Pineapple Chunks (20 oz.), Optional
- Cold Water

MMMMMMMMMMMMMMMMMMMMMMMMMMMMMMM

Methods:

1. Make pineapple chunk ice cubes a day in advance.
2. Place one pineapple chunk in each ice cube tray section, fill with water. Freeze.
3. Bring one quart of water to boil. Add loose tea to a tea filter bag and infuse in hot water.
4. Steep tea four minutes. Remove tea in the infuser or bag of tea and discard.
5. Add sugar until dissolved and stir well. Add pineapple juice and then add cold water to make 2 quarts. Stir well. Chill.
6. Serve over pre-made pineapple ice cubes.

(12) Blackberry Minty Sweet Iced Tea

Blackberries make a flavorful sweet tea that tastes like summer!

Yield: 2 Quarts

Preparation Time: 15 mins

List of Ingredients:

- One Quart Hot Water
- 8 teaspoons Black Tea
- ¾ to 1 ½ Cups Sugar (to Taste)
- 1 tablespoon Chopped Fresh Mint
- 2 – 16 oz. Packages Blackberries (fresh or frozen, thawed)
- Cold Water

MMMMMMMMMMMMMMMMMMMMMMMMMMMMMMM

Methods:

1. Combine blackberries and sugar in a large container, crush with a wooden spoon. Stir in crushed mint. Set aside.

2. Bring one quart of water to boil. Add loose tea to a tea filter bag and infuse in hot water. Steep tea four minutes. Remove tea in the infuser or bag of tea and discard.

3. Add your tea to your blackberry mixture and allow to stand at room temperature for about 1 hour.

4. Strain into a pitcher, discarding solids. Add cold water, stirring until sugar dissolves, to make 2 quarts. Chill.

5. Serve over ice.

(13) Peaches and Cream Iced Tea

If you love peach pie, then this iced tea is definitely for you.

Yield: 2 Quarts

Preparation Time: 15 mins.

List of Ingredients:

- 1 Quart Hot Water
- 8 Tablespoons White Peach Tea OR
- 8 teaspoons Black Peach Tea
- 1 Cup Light Brown Sugar
- 1 Quart Cold Water
- ½ Cup Half and Half OR Fresh Cream
- Fresh Peach Slices for Garnish (optional)

MMMMMMMMMMMMMMMMMMMMMMMMMMMMMMM

Methods:

1. Bring one quart of water to boil. Add tea to a tea filter bag and infuse in hot water. Steep tea for five minutes.
2. Remove tea in the infuser or bag of tea and discard. Add sugar and stir to dissolve. Add remaining quart of cold water. Chill.
3. Serve over ice and garnish with fresh peach slices. Add a little half and half to each glass to taste.
4. For a sweet touch, you can dip moist rims of glasses in additional brown sugar before pouring tea. (optional)

(14) Blueberry Lemon Iced Tea

Taste the flavors of summer with this Lemon Blueberry Iced Tea made with blueberries and fresh lemon juice.

Yield: 2 Quarts

Preparation Time: 15 mins.

List of Ingredients:

- One Quart Hot Water
- 8 teaspoons Black Tea
- 2 – 16 oz. Packages Frozen Blueberries
- 1 Cup Fresh Lemon Juice, Freshly Squeezed
- ½ to ¾ Cup Sugar, or Simple Syrup to Taste (optional)
- Cold Water

MMMMMMMMMMMMMMMMMMMMMMMMMMMMMMM

Methods:

1. Bring frozen blueberries and freshly squeezed juice to a boil in a saucepan over the medium heat.

2. Cook, stirring frequently, five minutes. Remove from heat. Pour lemon blueberry mixture through a fine wire-mesh strainer in to a bowl.

3. Use the back of a spoon to squeeze out the juice and discard solids.

4. Bring one quart of water to boil. Add loose tea to Takeya Iced Tea Maker Infuser OR to a tea filter bag and infuse in hot water.

5. Steep tea five minutes. Remove tea in the infuser or bag of tea and discard. Add sugar if desired and stir to dissolve.

6. Add lemon blueberry mixture. Add cold water to make two quarts and stir well. Chill.

7. Serve in glasses over ice and garnish with fresh lemon slices.

(15) Minty Tea Punch

A delicious punch to share at picnics, potlucks, and parties.

Yield: 2 Quarts

Preparation Time: 15 mins.

List of Ingredients:

- One Quart Hot Water
- 12 Mint Sprigs
- 8 teaspoons Black Tea
- 1Cup Orange Juice
- ¼ Cup Lemon Juice
- ½ Cup Sugar
- Cold Water
- Orange and Lemon Slices, Optional

MMMMMMMMMMMMMMMMMMMMMMMMMMMMMMMM

Methods:

1. Bring one quart of water to boil. Add loose tea and mint sprigs to a tea filter bag and infuse in hot water.
2. Steep tea four minutes. Remove tea and mint sprigs in the infuser or bag of tea and discard.
3. Stir in orange and lemon juices and sugar; stir until sugar is dissolved.
4. Add cold water to make 2 quarts and stir. Chill.
5. Serve over ice. Garnish with orange and lemon slices if desired.

(16) Cherry Vanilla Iced Tea

This blend of cherry with vanilla is exquisite!

Yield: 2 Quarts

Preparation Time: 15 mins.

List of Ingredients:

- One Quart Hot Water
- 8 teaspoons Black Tea
- 2 teaspoonss. Vanilla Extract
- 2 Cups Cherry Juice
- Sugar or Simple Syrup, to Taste (optional)
- One Quart Cold Water
- Maraschino Cherries for Garnish (optional)

MMMMMMMMMMMMMMMMMMMMMMMMMMMMMMMM

Methods:

1. Bring one quart of water to boil.
2. Add loose tea to a tea filter bag and infuse in hot water.
3. Steep tea four minutes. Remove tea in the infuser or bag of tea and discard. Add sugar if desired and stir to dissolve.
4. Add 2 cups cherry juice and 2 teaspoonss. vanilla extract and stir.
5. Add water to make 2 quarts. Chill.
6. Serve in glasses over ice. Garnish with maraschino cherries.

(17) Minty Peach Iced Tea

The fresh taste of mint blended with the sweet taste of peach tea makes for a very refreshing tea!

Yield: 2 Quarts

Preparation Time: 15 mins.

List of Ingredients:

- One Quart Hot Water
- 8 teaspoons Black Tea OR
- English Breakfast Tea
- 4 Ripe Peaches, cut into ½ inch pieces
- 1 Small Bunch Fresh Mint Sprigs
- Sugar or Simple Syrup, to Taste (optional)
- One Quart Cold Water

MMMMMMMMMMMMMMMMMMMMMMMMMMMMMMM

Methods:

1. Bring one quart of water to boil. Add loose tea to a tea filter bag and infuse in hot water.
2. Steep tea four minutes. Remove tea in the infuser or bag of tea and discard.
3. Add sugar if desired and stir to dissolve. Add peach slices and mint, let sit another five minutes.
4. Strain tea. Add remaining quart of cold water to strained tea. Chill.
5. Serve over ice and garnish with fresh peach slices and mint leaves.

(18) Citrus Iced Tea

Delightfully fresh and enjoyable, Citrus Tea revitalizes and quenches your thirst.

Yield: 2 Quarts

Preparation Time: 15 mins.

List of Ingredients:

- One Quart Hot Water
- 8 teaspoons Black Tea
- 8 Tablespoons sugar
- 1 Cinnamon Stick
- Freshly Squeezed Lemon Juice from 2 Lemons
- Slices of Oranges, Lemons, and/or Cucumbers
- Cold Water

MMMMMMMMMMMMMMMMMMMMMMMMMMMMMMMM

Methods:

1. Bring one quart of water to boil. Add loose tea to a tea filter bag and infuse in hot water. Steep tea four minutes.
2. Remove tea in the infuser or bag of tea and discard. Add cinnamon stick and sugar (if desired);
3. Stir until sugar dissolves. Let sit 1 hour.
4. Discard cinnamon stick. Stir in lemon juice. Add slices of oranges, lemons, and/or cucumbers. Add cold water to make 2 quarts and stir. Chill.
5. Serve over ice.

(19) Minty Iced Green Tea

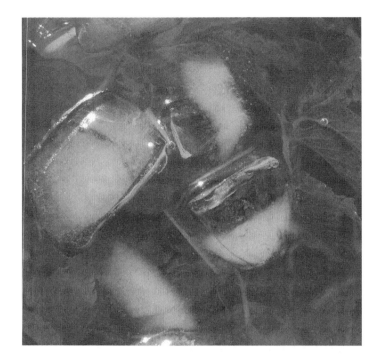

Iced Minty Green Tea is smooth and satisfying.

Yield: 2 Quarts

Preparation Time: 15 mins.

List of Ingredients:

- One Quart Hot Water
- 8 teaspoons Green Tea
- 1 Cup Fresh Mint Leaves, Crushed Gently
- Honey to Taste (optional)
- One Quart Cold Water

MMMMMMMMMMMMMMMMMMMMMMMMMMMMMMM

Methods:

1. Bring one quart of water to boil. Add loose tea and crushed mint leaves to a tea filter bag and infuse in hot water.
2. Steep tea and mint leaves for four minutes. Remove tea and mint leaves in the infuser or bag of tea and discard.
3. Add honey if desired and stir well. Add remaining quart of cold water and stir. Chill.
4. Serve over ice.

(20) Cranberry Mint Tea Lemonade

Your family will LOVE this tasteful and pretty tea!

Yield: 2 Quarts

Preparation Time: 15 mins

List of Ingredients:

- One Quart Hot Water
- 8 teaspoons Moroccan Mint Tea
- 1 Cup Cranberry Juice
- 1 Can Pink Lemonade Concentrate
- ½ cup to 1 cup Sugar, or Simple Syrup to Taste
- Slices of Lemon for Garnish
- Cold Water

MMMMMMMMMMMMMMMMMMMMMMMMMMMMMMMM

Methods:

1. Bring one quart of water to boil. Add loose tea to a tea filter bag and infuse in hot water.
2. Steep tea four minutes. Remove tea in the infuser or bag of tea and discard. Stir in sugar until dissolved.
3. Add cranberry juice and pink lemonade concentrate until well blended. Add cold water to make 2 quarts and stir. Chill.
4. Serve over ice and garnish with lemon slices.

(21) Mango Iced Tea

This delicious brew of luscious, sweet mango iced tea is perfect to quench your thirst on a warm, sunny day!

Yield: 2 Quarts

Preparation Time: 5 mins.

List of Ingredients:

- One Quart Hot Water
- 8 teaspoons Black Tea
- 2 Medium Mangoes (approx. 1 ½ - 2 Cups), Peeled and Chopped
- 1 teaspoon Lemon Juice, Freshly Squeezed
- Honey, Sugar, or Simple Syrup to Taste (optional)
- Mint Leaves and Lemon Slices for Garnish
- Cold Water

MMMMMMMMMMMMMMMMMMMMMMMMMMMMMM

Methods:

1. Puree mango in blender or food processor, set aside.
2. Bring one quart of water to boil. Add loose to a tea filter bag and infuse in hot water.
3. Steep tea four minutes. Remove tea from in the infuser or bag of tea and discard.
4. Add sweetener if desired and stir well. Add pureed mango, lemon juice, and tea to blender in batches and blend well.
5. Pour tea mixture into pitcher and fill to 2 quarts with cold water if needed. Stir well and chill.
6. Serve over ice and garnish with mint leaves and lemon slices.

(22) Cranberry-Raspberry Tea

Any easy and delicious recipe that is great for a sunny afternoon picnic or anytime, anywhere.

Yield: 2 Quarts

Preparation Time: 15 mins.

List of Ingredients:

- One Quart Hot Water
- 8 teaspoons Black Tea
- 1 Can (11.5 oz) Cranberry-Raspberry Juice Concentrate
- Cold Water
- Ice Cube with Raspberries Frozen Inside (optional, see page 3)
- Sugar or Simple Syrup to Taste (optional)

MMMMMMMMMMMMMMMMMMMMMMMMMMMMMMMMM

Methods:

1. Bring one quart of water to boil. Add loose tea to a tea filter bag and infuse in hot water.
2. Steep tea four minutes. Remove tea in the infuser or bag of tea and discard.
3. Stir in cranberry-raspberry juice concentrate until well blended. Add cold water to make 2 quarts and stir. Chill.
4. Serve over ice.

(23) Lavender Lemon Iced Tea

This mixture pairs with lemon to make a perfect iced tea.

Yield: 2 Quarts

Preparation Time: 15 mins.

List of Ingredients:

- One Quart Hot Water
- 8 teaspoons Green Tea
- 2 Sprigs Fresh Mint
- 2 teaspoons Dried Lemongrass or Lemon Balm
- 2 teaspoons Dried Lavender (food grade)
- Lemon Slices for Garnish (optional)
- Honey, Sugar, or Simple Syrup to Taste (optional)
- 1 Quart Cold Water

MMMMMMMMMMMMMMMMMMMMMMMMMMMMMMMM

Methods:

1. Bring one quart of water to boil. Add loose tea, dried lemongrass, and dried lavender to a tea filter bag and infuse in hot water.
2. Steep tea four minutes. Remove infuser or bag of tea.
3. Add sweetener if desired and stir well. Chill.
4. Serve over ice.

(24) Creamy Chai Iced Tea

Chai's spice is a perfect pick-me-up for a lazy summer afternoon and is a delicious culinary treat.

Yield: 2 Quarts

Preparation Time: 15 mins.

List of Ingredients:

- One Quart Hot Water
- 8 teaspoons Chai Tea
- Cinnamon Sticks
- One Quart Cold Water
- Sweetened Condensed Milk to taste

MMMMMMMMMMMMMMMMMMMMMMMMMMMMMMMMMM

Methods:

1. Bring one quart of water to boil. Add loose tea to a tea filter bag and infuse in hot water.
2. Steep tea four minutes. Remove tea in the infuser or bag of tea and discard. Add remaining quart of cold water and stir. Chill.
3. Serve over ice and add desired amount of sweetened condensed milk.
4. Garnish with cinnamon stick.

(25) Iced Tea Smoothie

Smoothies are a great way to start the day, so why not get all the health benefits of tea too!

Yield: 1 cup

Preparation Time: 15 mins.

List of Ingredients:

- One Cup of Water
- 4 Servings Tea Leaves
- One Medium Ripe Banana
- ½ Cup Ice Cubes
- Additional Fruit or Additives of Your Choice (optional)

MMMMMMMMMMMMMMMMMMMMMMMMMMMMMMMM

Methods:

1. Make a concentrated tea base by infusing 4 servings tea leaves with one cup of water and leaving to infuse overnight.
2. Remove tea leaves and discard. Chill.
3. Add prepared tea concentrate, ice and banana then any other additional additives to a blender and blend ingredients well.
4. Serve and enjoy.

(26) Ginger Honey Iced Tea

Ginger Honey Tea is a soothing elixir that boosts health and immunity.

Yield: 2 Quarts

Preparation Time: 15 mins.

List of Ingredients:

- One Quart Hot Water
- 8 teaspoons Black Tea
- 2 teaspoons Freshly Grated Ginger
- 1/3 Cup Honey
- One Quart Cold Water

MMMMMMMMMMMMMMMMMMMMMMMMMMMMMMMMM

Methods:

1. Bring one quart of water to boil. Add loose tea to a tea filter bag and infuse in hot water.
2. Steep tea four minutes. Remove tea in the infuser or bag of tea and discard.
3. Let cool until room temperature; add ginger and honey and stir well. Add remaining quart of cold water and stir. Chill.
4. Serve over ice.

(27) Iced Tea Shake

It is pure genius to turn iced tea into a fantastic and cooling shake!

Yield: 2 Quarts

Preparation Time: 15 mins.

List of Ingredients:

- One Quart Iced Tea, Chilled
- One Quart Ice Cream, Sorbet, Sherbet

MMMMMMMMMMMMMMMMMMMMMMMMMMMMMMMMMM

Methods:

1. Prepare your favorite iced tea by following your favorite recipe from this book.
2. In two batches, add half of the tea and half of the ice cream to a blender and blend well on high speed.
3. Serve immediately.

(28) Green Tea Soda

Green Tea Soda is a fizzy and fresh alternative to soda!

Yield: 2 Quarts

Preparation Time: 15 mins.

List of Ingredients:

- One Quart Hot Water
- 8 teaspoons Green Tea OR Moroccan Mint Tea
- 3 Tablespoons Honey or Sugar
- 4 Cups Assorted Fruit (Lime and/or Lemon Slices, Blueberries, Raspberries, and/or Peach Slices)
- 2 Tablespoons Snipped Fresh Mint (omit if using Moroccan Mint Tea)
- Flavored or Plain Sparkling Water

MMMMMMMMMMMMMMMMMMMMMMMMMMMMMMMM

Methods:

1. Bring one quart of water to boil. Add loose tea to a tea filter bag and infuse in hot water. Steep tea four minutes.
2. Remove tea in the infuser or bag of tea and discard.
3. Add honey or sugar and stir until well blended. Chill.
4. Fill glass halfway with tea mixture.
5. Add fruit and ice to each glass and fill glass with sparkling water.

(29) Honeydew Mint Iced Tea

Juicy honeydew melon adds a delightful and delicious twist to mint iced green tea.

Yield: 2 Quarts

Preparation Time: 15 mins.

List of Ingredients:

- One Quart Hot Water
- 8 teaspoons Green Tea
- 3 Cups Cubed, Peeled Honeydew Melon
- 1/3 cup Sugar
- 1 Cup Mint Leaves
- Cold Water

MMMMMMMMMMMMMMMMMMMMMMMMMMMMMMM

Methods:

1. Bring one quart of water to boil. Add loose tea to a tea filter bag and infuse in hot water.
2. Steep tea four minutes. Remove tea in the infuser or bag of tea and discard.
3. Meanwhile, bring mint, sugar and melon to a boil in a medium saucepan.
4. Reduce heat to low and simmer until melon is broken down, about 8 minutes.
5. Add to tea and let cool until room temperature; about 30 minutes. Refrigerate until cold, about 2 hours.
6. Strain through cheesecloth-lined wire mesh strainer, pressing solids gently. Add cold water to make 2 quarts if needed.
7. Serve over ice.

(30) Herbal Sun Tea

Lemon Ginger Herbal Tea is a caffeine-free herbal blend that is a breath of fresh air in a cup!

Yield: 2 Quarts

Preparation Time: 15 mins.

List of Ingredients:

- 8 Tablespoons Lemon Ginger Herbal Tea
- Honey, Sugar, or Simple Syrup to Taste
- 1 2-Qt. Jar or 2 1-Qt. Jars
- Cold Water
- Sunshine
- Lemon Slices (optional)

MMMMMMMMMMMMMMMMMMMMMMMMMMMMMMM

Methods:

1. Place Lemon Ginger Herbal Tea into tea filter bags or an infuser. (Divide into two bags if using two 1-Qt. jars.)
2. Fill jar(s) with cold water and cover.
3. Steep in direct sunlight for 2 hours. Strain tea if necessary.
4. Add honey or sugar to taste, stir well.
5. Serve over ice.

About the Author

A native of Indianapolis, Indiana, Valeria Ray found her passion for cooking while she was studying English Literature at Oakland City University. She decided to try a cooking course with her friends and the experience changed her forever. She enrolled at the Art Institute of Indiana which offered extensive courses in the culinary Arts. Once Ray dipped her toe in the cooking world, she never looked back.

When Valeria graduated, she worked in French restaurants in the Indianapolis area until she became the head chef at one of the 5-star establishments in the area. Valeria's attention to taste and visual detail caught the eye of a local business person who expressed an interest in publishing her recipes. Valeria began her secondary career authoring cookbooks and e-books which she tackled with as much talent and gusto as her first career. Her passion for food leaps off the page of her books which have colourful anecdotes and stunning pictures of dishes she has prepared herself.

Valeria Ray lives in Indianapolis with her husband of 15 years, Tom, her daughter, Isobel and their loveable Golden Retriever, Goldy. Valeria enjoys cooking special dishes in her large, comfortable kitchen where the family gets involved in preparing meals. This successful, dynamic chef is an inspiration to culinary students and novice cooks everywhere.

Author's Afterthoughts

Thank you for Purchasing my book and taking the time to read it from front to back. I am always grateful when a reader chooses my work and I hope you enjoyed it!

With the vast selection available online, I am touched that you chose to be purchasing my work and take valuable time out of your life to read it. My hope is that you feel you made the right decision.

I very much would like to know what you thought of the book. Please take the time to write an honest and informative review on Amazon.com. Your experience and opinions will be of great benefit to me and those readers looking to make an informed choice.

With much thanks,

Valeria Ray